First published in The United States by **Holland Brown Books, LLC** 2009

The Anchor Building
2509 Portland Avenue
Louisville
Kentucky 40212
USA

www.hollandbrownbooks.com

ISBN 13: 978-0-9797006-2-0
ISBN 10: 0-9797006-2-0
Library of Congress Control Number: 2009932626

Louisville Counts! A Children's Counting & Art Book
2nd Edition

By Gill Holland
Edited by Stephanie Brothers

Contributing Artists

Chris Radtke, Nico Jorcino, Jacob Heustis, Cynthia Reynolds, Natasha Sud, Monica Mahoney, Gibbs Rounsavall, Bryce Hudson, Amanda Bishop, J.B. Wilson, McKinley Moore, Julius Friedman, Lloyd Kelly, Russel Hulsey, Billy Hertz, Letitia Quesenberry, Thea Lura, Ashley Cecil, Sarah Lyon, Valerie Fuchs, Skylar Smith, and Stephen Irwin.

Supplementary Photography by Rachel Seed
Graphic Design by Ty Kreft
Cover and Text Illustrations by Amanda Bishop

The moral right of the authors and artists has been reserved.

Typeset and Printed in Canada.

For Cora

LOUISVILLE COUNTS!
a children's counting & art book

by **Gill Holland**

edited by **Stephanie Brothers**

With generous contributions from these **Louisville artists:**

Chris Radtke (0), Nico Jorcino (1), Jacob Heustis (2), Cynthia Reynolds (3), Natasha Sud (4), Monica Mahoney (5), Gibbs Rounsavall (6), Bryce Hudson (7), Amanda Bishop (8), J.B. Wilson (9), McKinley Moore (10), Julius Friedman (11), Lloyd Kelly (12), Russel Hulsey (13), Billy Hertz (14), Letitia Quesenberry (15), Thea Lura (16), Ashley Cecil (17), Sarah Lyon (18), Valerie Fuchs (19), Skylar Smith (20), and Stephen Irwin (21).

Supplementary photography by Rachel Seed.

Copious gratitude to our outstanding graphic designer, Ty Kreft.

Thanks to everyone that played a part in the creation of Louisville Counts!

All proceeds from all sales of this book, as well as half of the sales of corresponding artworks, go directly to Art Sparks Interactive Gallery, the children's gallery at The Speed Art Museum.

O is for the Louisville **LOOP** that forms a 100 mile circle trail around the city.

1 RIVER

Louisville is on the banks of the Mighty OHIO RIVER.

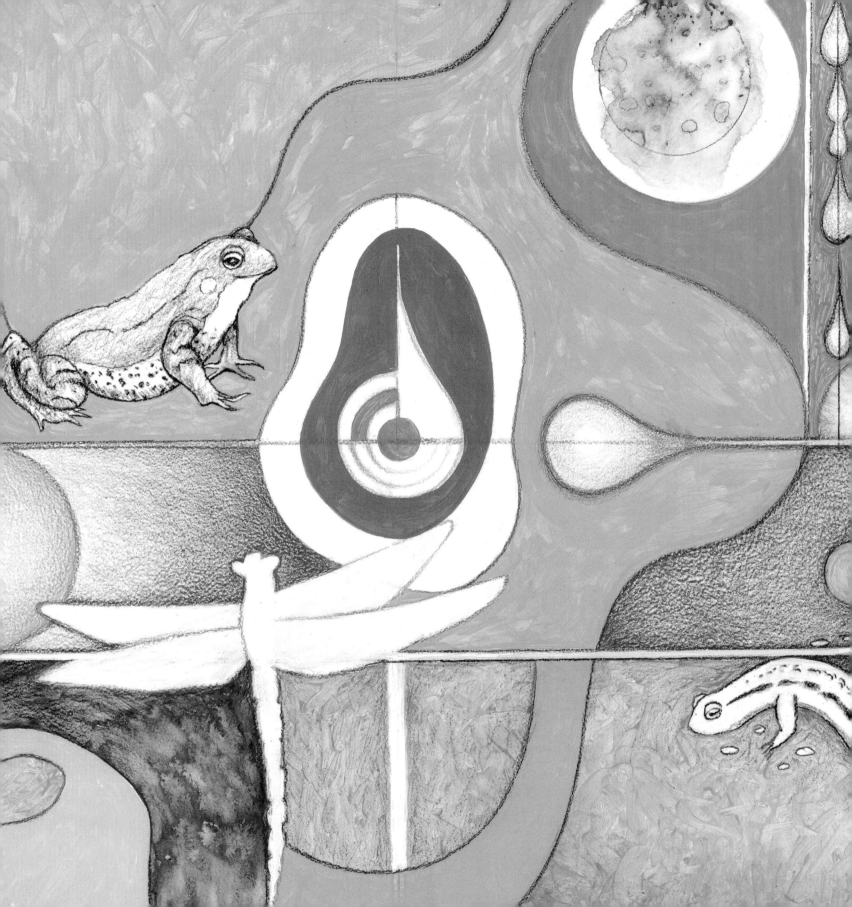

Churchill Downs is famous for its **(2) TWIN SPIRES.** Every year thousands come to Louisville for the Kentucky Derby.

3 **leaves of the FLEUR DE LIS,** the symbol of Louisville. It graces our flag and our seal.

4 BASES

at Slugger Field—

first,

second, third...

HOME RUN!

5 PLAYERS take the court for the UNIVERSITY of Louisville **Cardinal** basketball team!

FREDERICK OLMSTED designed New York's CENTRAL PARK and then 6 MAJOR PARKS here in Louisville. Can you find the names?

7 EASTER EGGS.

Everyone loves sweets from Muth's Candy **on historic** East Market Street.

They have been making candy since 1926.

Louisville has 8 SISTER CITIES

throughout the WORLD:

Jiujiang in China, Montpellier in France, Perm in Russia, Quito in Ecuador, Tamale in Ghana, Leeds in the United Kingdom La Plata in Argentina, and Mainz in Germany.

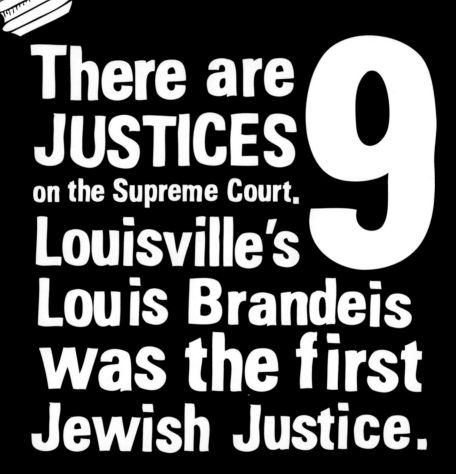

There are JUSTICES 9 on the Supreme Court. Louisville's Louis Brandeis was the first Jewish Justice.

The Supreme Court of the United StatesThe Supreme Court of the United States is the highest court in the land and the only part of the federal judiciary specifically required by the Constitution. The Constitution does not stipulate the number of Supreme Court Justices; the number is set instead by Congress. There have been as few as six, but since 1869, there have been nine Justices, including one Chief Justice. All Justices are nominated by the President, confirmed by the Senate, and hold their offices under life tenure. Since Justices do not have to run or campaign for re-election, they are thought to be insulated from political pressure when deciding cases. Justices may remain in office until they resign, pass away, or are impeached and convicted by Congress.The Court's caseload is almost entirely appellate in nature, and the Court's decisions cannot be appealed to any authority, as it is the final judicial arbiter in the United States on matters of federal law. However, the Court may consider appeals from the highest state courts or from federal appellate courts. The Court also has original jurisdiction in cases involving ambassadors and other diplomats, and in cases between states.Although the Supreme Court may hear an appeal on any question of law provided it has jurisdiction, it usually does not hold trials. Instead, the Court's task is to interpret the meaning of a law, to decide whether a law is relevant to a particular set of facts, or to rule on how a law should be applied. Lower courts are obligated to follow the precedent set by the Supreme Court when rendering decisions.In almost all instances, the Supreme Court does not hear appeals as a matter of right; instead, parties must petition the Court for a writ of certiorari. It is the Court's custom and practice to "grant cert" if four of the nine Justices decide that they should hear the case. Of the approximately 7,500 requests for certiorari filed each year, the Court usually grants cert to fewer than 150. These are typically cases that the Court considers sufficiently important to require their review; a common example is the occasion when two or more of the federal courts of appeals have ruled differently on the same question of federal law. If the Court grants certiorari, Justices accept legal briefs from the parties to the case, as well as from amicus curiae, or "friends of the court." These can include industry trade groups, academics, or even the U.S. government itself. Before issuing a ruling, the Supreme Court usually hears oral arguments, where the various parties to the suit present their arguments and the Justices ask them questions. If the case involves the federal government, the Solicitor General of the United States presents arguments on behalf of the United States. The Justices then hold private conferences, make their decision, and (often after a period of several months) issue the Court's opinion, along with any dissenting arguments that may have been written.The Judicial ProcessArticle III of the Constitution of the United States guarantees that every person accused of wrongdoing has the right to a fair trial before a competent judge and a jury of one's peers.The Fourth, Fifth, and Sixth Amendments to the Constitution provide additional protections for those accused of a crime. These include:A guarantee that no person shall be deprived of life, liberty, or property without the due process of law Protection against being tried for the same crime twice ("double jeopardy") The right to a speedy trial by an impartial jury The right to cross-examine witnesses, and to call witnesses to support their case The right to legal representation The right to avoid self-incrimination Protection from excessive bail, excessive fines, and cruel and unusual punishments Criminal proceedings can be conducted under either state or federal law, depending on the nature and extent of the crime. A criminal legal procedure typically begins with an arrest by a law enforcement officer. If a grand jury chooses to deliver an indictment, the accused will appear before the judge and be formally charged with a crime, at which time he or she may enter a plea. The defendant is given time to review all the evidence in the case and to build a legal argument. Then, the case is brought to trial and decided by a jury. If the defendant is determined to be not guilty of the crime, the charges are dismissed. Otherwise, the judge determines the sentence, which can include prison time, a fine, or even execution. Civil cases are similar to criminal ones, but instead of arbitrating between the state and a person or organization, they deal with disputes between individuals or organizations. If a party believes that it has been wronged, it can file suit in civil court to attempt to have that wrong remedied through an order to cease and desist, alter behavior, or award monetary damages. After the suit is filed and evidence is gathered and presented by both sides, a trial proceeds as in a criminal case. If the parties involved waive their right to a jury trial, the case can be decided by a judge; otherwise, the case is decided and damages awarded by a jury.After a criminal or civil case is tried, it may be appealed to a higher court — a federal court of appeals or state appellate court. A litigant who files an appeal, known as an "appellant," must show that the trial court or administrative agency made a legal error that affected the outcome of the case. An appellate court makes its decision based on the record of the case established by the trial court or agency — it does not receive additional evidence or hear witnesses. It may also review the factual findings of the trial court or agency, but typically may only overturn a trial outcome on factual grounds if the findings were "clearly erroneous." If a defendant is found not guilty in a criminal proceeding, he or she cannot be retried on the same set of facts. Federal appeals are decided by panels of three judges. The appellant presents legal arguments to the panel, in a written document called a "brief." In the brief, the appellant tries to persuade the judges that the trial court made an error, and that the lower decision should be reversed. On the other hand, the party defending against the appeal, known as the "appellee" or "respondent," tries in its brief to show why the trial court decision was correct, or why any errors made by the trial court are not significant enough to affect the outcome of the case.The court of appeals usually has the final word in the case, unless it sends the case back to the trial court for additional proceedings. In some cases the decision may be reviewed en banc — that is, by a larger group of judges of the court of appeals for the circuit. A litigant who loses in a federal court of appeals, or in the highest court of a state, may file a petition for a "writ of certiorari," which is a document asking the Supreme Court to review the case. The Supreme Court, however, is not obligated to grant review. The Court typically will agree to hear a case only when it involves a new and important legal principle, or when two or more federal appellate courts have interpreted a law differently. (There are also special circumstances in which the Supreme Court is required by law to hear an appeal.) When the Supreme Court hears a case, the parties are required to file written briefs and the Court may hear oral argument.

10 GLASS SCULPTURES. Many artists who blow glass live in Louisville.

11 CITIES...

Only eleven cities in the United States have all the major cultural institutions. Louisville has:

Actors Theatre, Louisville Ballet, Kentucky Opera, Louisville Orchestra and Speed Art Museum.

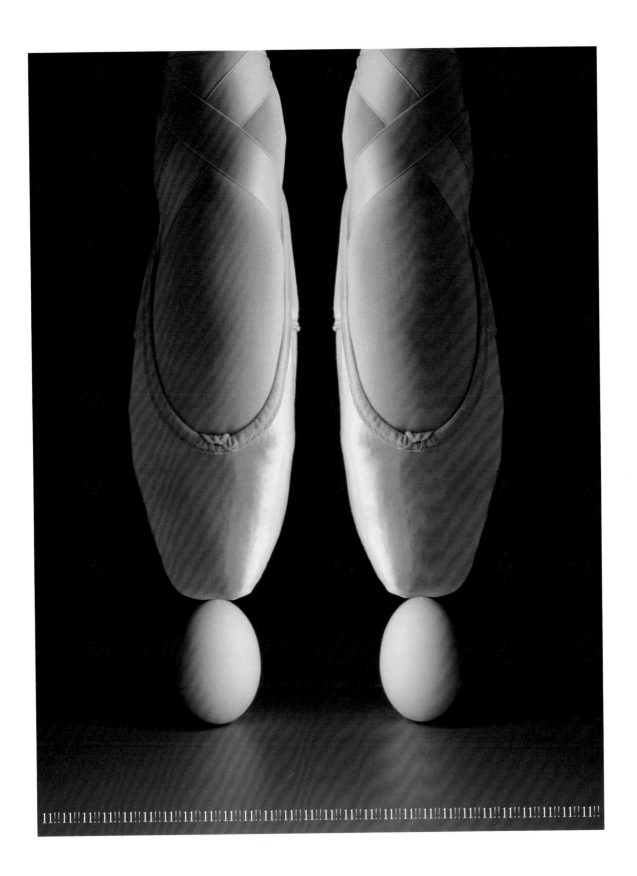
11!!11!!11!!11!!11!!11!!11!!11!!11!!11!!11!!11!!11!!11!!11!!11!!11!!11!!11!!11!!11!!11!!11!!11!!11!!11!!11!!11!!11!!11!!11!!

12 is for the HORSES

which munch on the bluegrass around Louisville **and all over Kentucky.**

There are letters in "Happy Birthday," **13** a song written by the Hill Sisters in 1893 in Louisville. Count the cakes!

happy birthday

14 BASEBALL BATS... the famed Louisville **Slugger** is made in downtown Louisville.

There are **15** ROUNDS in a boxing match... unless you faced **Louisville's Muhammad Ali.** Then you probably didn't make it that long!

Louisville was named for the FRENCH KING LOUIS 16 because his soldiers helped America in the REVOLUTIONARY WAR.

Louisville is the **17**th largest city in America

There are **18** H◯LES on a golf course. In 2008 Louisville's Valhalla Golf Club hosted the Ryder Cup, an international tournament.

In the late 19th century, Thomas Edison

lived on Washington Street in Louisville's historic **Butchertown.** He invented the light bulb.

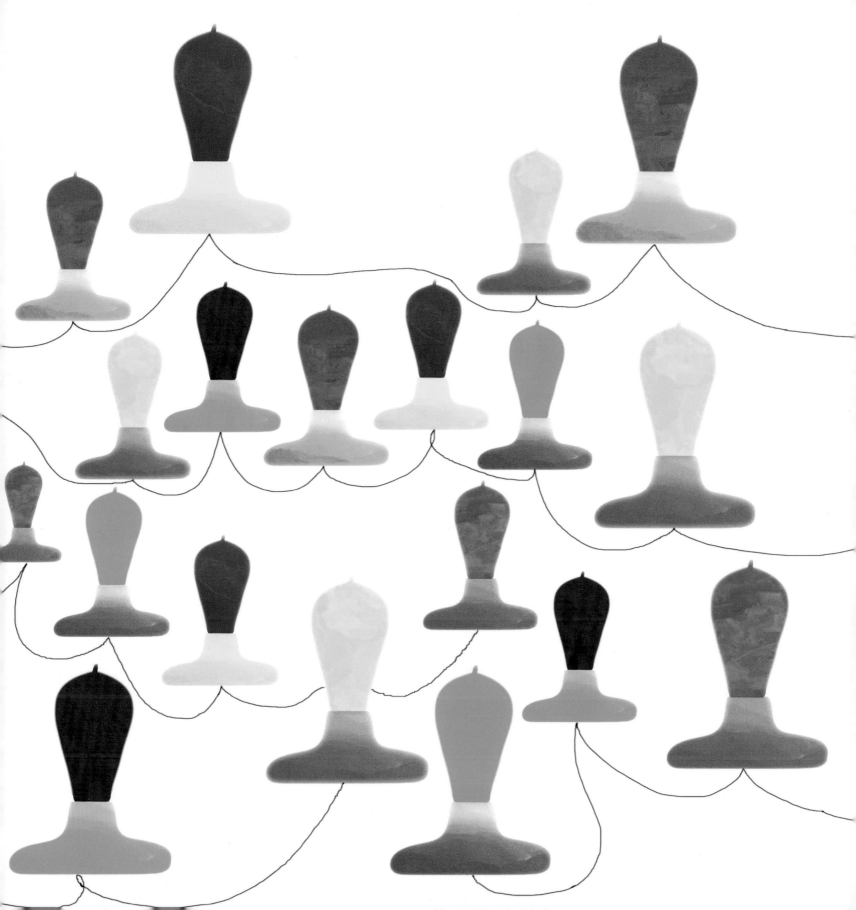

Most disco balls in the USA are made on Baxter Avenue. Can you find all 20?

21c, the first ART HOTEL in the world, is located on Louisville's historic West Main Street.

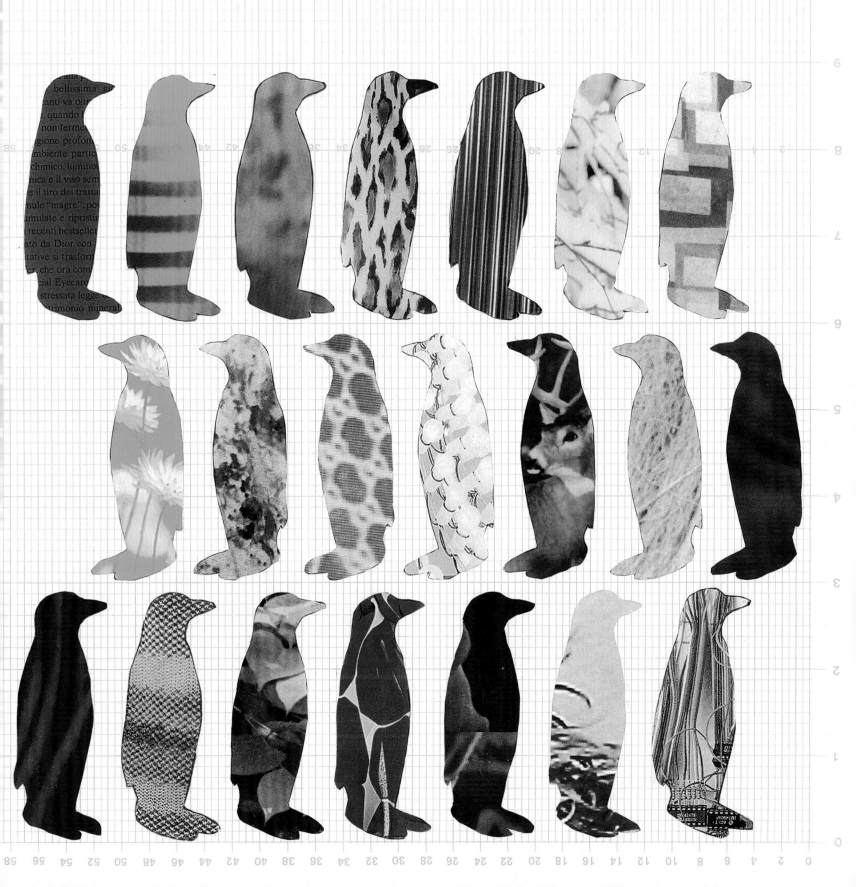

Louisville Artists

0 - Chris Radtke

Chris Radtke is an artist whose work has been shown internationally. She is a former member of the Board of Governors of the Speed Art Museum and is currently co-chairing the Mayor's Advisory Committee on Public Art and is a member of New Art Collectors.

1 - Nico Jorcino

Argentinean, born 1966. Living and working in Louisville since 2002. Inspired by his intimate experiences as an immigrant and his interest in architecture and urban planning, Jorcino has created a body of work in which he explores the relationship between his experiences and his interests through art.

2 - Jacob Heustis

Jacob Heustis lives and makes things.

3 - Cynthia Reynolds

Cynthia Reynolds is a native of Louisville. She studied at Centre College, Kansas City Art Institute, and the University of Washington in Seattle, where she earned her Master of Fine Arts in Ceramics in 1997. She was an artist-in-residence at Louisville Stoneware from 2003 to 2005, and was awarded a Kentucky Arts Council Al Smith Individual Artist Fellowship in 2006 and a Kentucky Foundation for Women Artist Enrichment grant in 2008.

4 - Natasha Sud

Russian native Natasha Sud grew up in Louisville and attended the University of Louisville for photography. It was in Los Angeles, where she lived for seven years, that she started making mixed media collages on wood. She moved back to Louisville in 2005 where she continues to pursue her creative vision. She has been in various group and solo shows in both California and Kentucky.

5 - Monica Mahoney

Monica Mahoney is an artist born, raised, and trying to count in Louisville (even though she is dyslexic). She and her partner Schoen love cheering on the U of L women's basketball team and ALL the Cardinals.

Louisville Artists

6 - Gibbs Rounsavall

Gibbs Rounsavall is a contemporary artist living and working in Louisville. His work can be found in public, private and corporate collections.

7 - Bryce Hudson

Born in 1979 and a Louisville resident since 1999, Bryce Hudson is a visual artist who believes that experimentation and evolution are essential to the development of all artists. Each exhibition features new paintings and prints, as he constantly reinvents his definition of alternative art spaces and studios. His work has garnered attention from venues and collections that span the globe.

8 - Amanda Bishop

Since Amanda was a small child, she has dedicated herself to the pursuit of making art. From painting classes in elementary school, to a degree in Visual Arts from the University of Washington in Seattle, to her present day career in illustration, she has dabbled in most media and enjoyed them all.

9 - J.B. Wilson

J.B. Wilson is a Kentuckian currently living and working in Louisville. He is a founder of and represented by Art Ecology Gallery. He is a very versatile artist working in many media. He describes his latest work as "contemporary digital pop."

10 - McKinley Moore

McKinley Moore is originally from Inez, a town of 600 people in Eastern Kentucky. He graduated in 2003 with a BA in Studio Art from Centre College where he studied glass-blowing under Stephen Rolfe Powell. Since then, McKinley has worked and taught in glass-blowing studios in Louisville, Chicago, and New Orleans. He is a founding board member of the local sustainable arts organization, Ohio Valley Creative Energy.

11 - Julius Friedman

Julius Friedman is a graphic designer, photographer, artist, and owner of the design firm Images, specializing in cultural, non-profit, and corporate design. He co-owns Chapman Friedman Gallery, which represents contemporary regional, national, and international artists.

Louisville Artists

12 – Lloyd Kelly

Painter Lloyd Kelly was born in 1946 in New Orleans, Louisiana.

He received a BA in Political Science from Louisiana State University in 1970; a BFA in Drawing from the University of Nebraska in 1973; a MFA in Printmaking from the Instituto Allende, University of Guanajuato, San Miguel de Allende, Mexico in 1975, and a MFA in Creative Writing in 2003 from Spalding University. He completed studies in Museum Curation at the University of Colorado, Boulder and museum studies at the Louvre Museum and Tate Gallery. He has exhibited extensively throughout the world.

13 – Russel Hulsey

Russel Hulsey's current artistic endeavors focus upon time-based video works, interactive technologies, and multi-sensory immersive installations. Hulsey has been an active artist since 1997, working in drawing, painting, photography, and a wide array of varied electronic media.

14 – Billy Hertz

Billy Hertz has been an integral part of Louisville's art scene as both an artist and gallery owner. Involved in the germination and cultivation of Louisville's downtown renaissance, Billy was recently awarded the prestigious Ida Lee Willis Memorial Award for Service to Preservation.

He commands equal respect as a painter. His work is included in major collections throughout the region and world, including the Museo del Tulle in Italy, the Perm Picture Gallery Museum in Russia, the Midwest Museum of American Art in Elkhart, Indiana and several corporate and private collections from coast to coast.

15 – Letitia Quesenberry

Letitia Quesenberry was born in Louisville where she currently lives and works.

She was recently awarded an Efroymson Contemporary Arts Fellowship and a residency at the UCROSS Foundation in Wyoming. Her drawings are included in the Drawing Center's Viewing Program and the Flat Files at Pierogi Gallery.

Louisville Artists

16 - Thea Lura

Thea Lura, a South Dakota native, lives and works in Louisville. She paints, types, jewels, serves the public, and avoids growing up.

17 - Ashley Cecil

Louisville native Ashley Cecil has been creating art ever since discovering that her mom's favorite lipstick made a great oil pastel. As a teenager, painting was an intriguing challenge and a skill to be mastered, which led to her formal art education and years of professional experience.

Cecil juggles a broad array of work related to the visual arts and activism, most significantly by authoring "The Painting Activist" (www.ashleycecil.com), an online journal of her illustrative paintings that promote social and environmental causes.

18 - Sarah Lyon

Sarah's dad Jim bought a camera to take photographs of her when she was a kid growing up in Louisville. When she was eighteen, Sarah borrowed that camera to start taking her own photographs, and her dad hasn't seen it since.

19 - Valerie Fuchs

Valerie Sullivan Fuchs is an artist who currently works with video, sound, video installation and sculpture. She has exhibited extensively throughout the United States and abroad, and has been awarded a number of grants and fellowships. Also a writer, she has been published in numerous publications.

20 - Skylar Smith

Skylar Smith has a Bachelor of Fine Art from Maryland Institute College of Art, as well as a Master of Fine Art from the School of the Art Institute of Chicago. She has exhibited work in Louisville, Chicago, and abroad in Delhi and Rajasthan, India. Smith is a Professor of Fine Art and Art History at the University of Louisville, and also teaches at the Jefferson Community College and Luther Luckett Correctional Complex.

21 - Stephen Irwin

Stephen Irwin is a native Kentuckian. He lives and works in Louisville. He is in the permanent collections of the Speed Art Museum and 21c Museum. He is represented by Zephyr Gallery Louisville, Invisible Exports in New York and Jonathan Ferrara Gallery in New Orleans.